INTEGRITY OF
CHRISTIANITY
CHARACTER DEVELOPMENT

Abiding Process – **St. John 15:7**

Terri'Ann Williams Howard, M.S.

WESTBOW
PRESS®
A DIVISION OF THOMAS NELSON
& ZONDERVAN

contact: terrieann14@gmail.com
Mailing: World of Girls and Boys Empowerment Mentorship Co, Inc.
P.O. Box 411
Buffalo, NY 14215

Scripture taken from the King James Version of the Bible.

WestBow Press books may be ordered through booksellers or by contacting:

WestBow Press
A Division of Thomas Nelson & Zondervan
1663 Liberty Drive
Bloomington, IN 47403
www.westbowpress.com
1 (866) 928-1240

ISBN: 978-1-9736-1291-9 (sc)

Print information available on the last page.

WestBow Press rev. date: 03/23/2018

DEDICATION

This book is dedicated to my darling husband Maurice. Thank you for

Being an example of the fruit of Integrity. Also, my wonderful parents

Dillard and Marion Williams Jr., for teaching our family about the

Value of honesty and hard work. To my awesome biological children; Genetino, Te'Anna, & Tonyamarie, you all have grown so much. I am so Godly proud of you. Continue training yourselves to live a life of Integrity in all that you do.

Many thanks to my sisters and my brother Stephen, you all are so special to me.

My family, I love you all so much!

CONTENTS

ACKNOWLEDGEMENTS

This book has been a very long project for me. I have endured bitter and sweet moments. When I began writing this book, my dear mother contracted colon cancer. Unfortunately, she later passed from this life. It was truly my loss, but her gain. After my mothers' death, I would constantly hear her words, "Terri, carry on". These were the words that she would say to my quite often. After her passing, I semi lost the desire to complete the book. She was my shero, and always validated me. Finally, after many years of allowing this book to sit on the shelf, one day I knew that it was time to bounce back. Forcing myself to get back into the race, refocusing on my dreams and aspirations. I am grateful for those who have rejected me, misunderstood me and despised my steadfast tenacity. Those times have been a blessing to me. Today, I can truly say that each trial and test was helpful and a learning experience. Through it all, I was provoked to abide in the presence of the Lord. The abiding process is where I continue to learn about the integrity of Christianity. Jesus said, "If you abide in me, and my words abide in you, then you can ask what you will, and it shall be done of the father." St John 15:7

PREFACE

I am learning that the integrity of Christianity is the heart and character of God. According to the holy bible, it is Gods' desire for us to possess a heart that entails truth. (Psalm 51:6). I have researched many biblical accounts in the bible as it pertains to integrity. The accounts, set the foundation for the premise of this book. To share just a few of them; in the story of Abraham and Abimelech; Abraham told Abimelech that Sarah was his sister. However, she was his wife. His motive was to deceive the king. In actuality she was his half-sister and wife. He did not tell the truth because of fear. Abimelech could pursue Sarah if she was a single lady, and not married. Abraham's deception was not pleasing to God.

Later that night when Abimelech went to sleep, the Lord God visited him in a dream. God told him that Sarah was Abraham's wife. He also told him that he would die, if he touched her. When he awakened, he had a choice to make. Abimelech made the wise choice, which was integrity. He decided not to pursue Abraham's wife. (Genesis Chp.20). There is a gentleman in the bible named Solomon. He was given a charge from God. The charge was to obey God by remaining in covenant, and making righteous choices. He was instructed not to involve himself with ungodly affairs. Because they would separate him from his covenant with God, (1st Kings Chp.9).

"If thou wilt walk before me as David thy father walked,

with integrity of heart, and in uprightness to do according to all that I have commanded thee; and wilt keep my statues and judgments, then will I establish the throne of thy kingdoms upon Israel forever as I had promised to David thy father. Solomon would be privy to the thrones of the kingdom, only if he chose to obey the orders of God. He was instructed not to serve, follow or worship other Gods'. If Solomon chose to disobey the instructions of the Lord, he then would be cut off, and put out of the land of promise.

Job was considered an upright man. A person with integrity. "The Lord said to Satan, have you considered my servant Job? That there is none like him in the earth; a perfect and upright man. One who feareth God, and eschewed evil, and still holdeth fast his integrity."

(Job Chapter 2). David the Psalmist, he spoke these words unto God. "Judge me oh Lord; for I have walked in mine integrity. I have trusted also in the Lord, therefore I will not slide".

INTRODUCTION

T he integrity of Christianity is a short read. The book is designed to provoke and challenge us all to embrace a life style of Integrity. The book outlines biblical standards and stories. All of the scriptures are cited from the King James Version Bible.

As we examine our global society, the challenge at hand is waiting to see, who will hold true to integrity for the people. Subsequently, meeting the needs of our communities, country, and our world at large. Unfortunately, when we turn on our news and social media, we encounter character flaws with many systems that are in place. We have witnessed a lack of integrity within our churches, homes, schools, and government.

I am very happy, with being a Born Again Christian Believer. It's exciting to know that the Holy Spirit is my guide. For many years, until now, the Lord has quickened my spirit about the standards of Christianity, as it pertains to integrity. While looking over my life, I have developed and grown to a place in my relationship with the Lord, to understand that integrity must become a vital part of my life. For many years I had fallen into the temptation of wanting to please everyone, in hopes of being accepted. Allowing myself to compromise the standards of the Holy Scriptures. Within my heart, I knew that I was out of harmony with Gods plan for my life. From my experience, being out of harmony with God is a very lonely feeling.

Well, sit back relax, and enjoy the book. You will be inspired on new dimensions to embrace new levels of harmony with our Lord.

ABOUT THE AUTHOR

Terri' Ann is an ordained Minister & Community outreach Pastor. Her ministerial call and passion is to help to guide and empower young ladies. She is a longtime community activist for young ladies, for over twenty years. She has started pageants in the buffalo area that focuses on young ladies making a difference. She is the founder of the Young Ladies of Dignity Pageant and the Debutants of Divinity Pageants. She is the President and CEO of her company, which is the World of Girls and Boys Empowerment, Mentorship Co, Inc. Along with being a School Counselor in the Buffalo Schools District.

She is married to her amazing husband Maurice. Terri' Ann has three outstanding children. They are all college graduates. Their names are Genetino, Te'Anna and Tonyamarie. She has obtained many degrees. From Houghton Liberal Arts College, she has a Bachelor's Degree in Psychology and Biblical Studies. Her Masters' Degree is from Canisius College, School of Human Services and Counseling. Also a Masters' Degree in Christian Counseling from Jacksonville Theological Seminary, along with her _ministerial ordained_ license.

She is an educator, a counselor and a profound inspirational conference speaker empowering females on spiritual and personal development.

Terri' Ann learned the value of good character and hard work from her wonderful parents Dillard and Marion Williams Jr. She has six sisters and one brother. Her favorite word in life is Integrity.

CHAPTER 1

TEMPERANCE
(Identifying the Breech Places)

Wow! Look at me, I am moving forward towards success in many areas of my life. I am pursuing a great career in cosmetics and counseling. Perhaps searching for the finer things in this present world; such as cars, homes, money, friendships, vacations, and more will possibly give me the prestige I am looking for.

We all search for security on many levels. However, there will be times when gaining status and prestige by having material things will not bring complete satisfaction.

Perhaps, this scenario of success reminds you of yourself, and others who are striving for the totem pole of being acknowledged through a prestigious job, and a life of no lack. In as much, as this scenario may fit you or someone that you know; then reading this chapter will bring perspective, and an awareness of the need for temperance.

Temperance is having self-restraints. Because something or someone looks good, that does not mean it is necessarily good for you. Remember the story of King Abraham, and Abimelech?

Abraham was not honest with Abimelech. Abraham did not walk in the integrity of Gods standards and expectations. He was driven by fear, and the possibility of being killed, if he had told the truth regarding he and Sara's relationship. *You see, He and Sarah had what some would consider an extramarital affair. However, it was a bit more complicated than that.*

Abimelech later found out the truth. According to the bible, God appeared in his dream. The Lord told Abimelech the truth. Sarah was in deed Abraham's wife, and also his half- sister. After he heard the truth, he now had to make a decision. Either to ignore the truth or obey the Lord. While he pondered on his decision, he finally decided to choose truth. Integrity was the best choice. Had he not chosen to do the right thing, his life would have been expunged. God told him that he would die. Have you ever ignored the consequence of what could happen, if you did not take the road of integrity? The scripture states, "We are bought with a price, and our lives are not our own." (1ˢᵗ Corinthians 6:20).

David the Psalmist said, "Judge me Lord, for I have walked in mine integrity. I have trusted also in the Lord; therefore, I shall not slide" (Psalm 26:1). The words of Jesus, went like this; "You shall know the truth, and the truth shall make you free" (St. John 8:32) It is quite evident that there will be times in our lives when the moment of truth is painful. I can recall, when I was a little girl, and my mother said, "please don't touch the stove". That never worked with me. Because I was a very curious child, and would take the risk anyways.

I touched the stove, and the surging pain of the heat was horrific, along with the butt whoppin' that I later received from my mom because I was disobedient. It was just as painful. Disobedience carries a lot of regret. It is best to obey God, and receive the full blessings of grace. "Obedience is better than Sacrifice" (1ˢᵗ Samuel 15:22). Just like the Prophet Moses, he chose to suffer with the people of God and obey Gods' orders, than to enjoy the pleasures of sin for a season (Hebrews 11:24).

I believe when seasons of trials and tests come, that they are for us to discover what is doormat in our lives. Areas that are not submitted unto God.

Many times when we are obedient to the word of God according to the bible, sometimes persecution follows our obedience. Three of my favorite brothers in the bible are the three Hebrew Boys. Their names are Shadrack, Meshack and Abednego. They were challenged with the choice of bowing to the king's false god, or being thrown into a fiery furnace for not obeying the kings decree. obeying the Holy God of Israel.

Facing the possibility of death did not frighten them. They knew that they were serving a faithful God. Anyways, they chose not to bow to the false god. So, they were punished, and thrown into the fiery furnace. Our God was faithful, and rescued them. (Daniel 3:16 – 18). They are true examples of temperance through a life of integrity. It is important for us to train ourselves not to fret. Our God is faithful! Our brother Peter acknowledged trials in this vein; "Think it not strange concerning the fiery trial, which has come to try you, (1st Peter 4:12). In the midst of our fiery trial God has given us the power and authority over the situation." For the weapons of our warfare are not carnal, but mighty through God. To the pulling down of strong holds. (2nd Corinthians 10:4-5). Many times we do not understand some things. However, the scripture states, "Trust in the Lord, with all of our heart, and lean not to our own understanding" (Proverbs 3:5)

Paul the Apostle, had a thorn in his flesh. This was very painful for him. I believe the thorn was put there as a constant reminder. At one point in Paul's life he was very arrogant and self-willed. If God has to allow situations to tame us, I know he will. Many times Paul asked God to please remove the pain in his flesh. (2nd Corinthians 12:8). The Lord chose to keep it there. I have always looked at this situation with Paul, as a reminder, that God will allow us to be subdued if necessary. The lord wants to be in control of our lives. In essence, I believe God was hoping Paul would come to understand the importance of the abiding process. Our lives are so out of order when we are not being accountable to our creator. I do not like being out of order according to the scriptures. When I am out of order I have no harmony with God. That is a horrible feeling.

Sin separates us from God. It all started in the garden with Adam and Eve. (Genesis chap 3)

Let us pause for a moment, please close your eyes. Now think about these biblical words – "He that cometh to God must believe that he is, and that he is a rewarder of them that diligently seek him" (Hebrews 11:6).

Now say it again, aloud with your eyes closed and insert your name in the scripture verse. Training ourselves to seek the Lord, should be our daily focus. After all God is our creator, and knows about everything. Also about everyone else. There are no secrets with God.

From my personal experience; the Lord has revealed secrets to me. God has allowed me to hear the conversations of others in my dreams, while sleeping. I was forewarned of the decisions they were planning. When we walk closely with God, secrets can be revealed just as it was revealed to Abimelech, regarding Abraham and Sarah.

Gods' timing is always perfect. Galatians 6:7, states' "Let us not be weary in well doing, for in due season we shall reap if we faint not." I love this agreement between the Lord God, and those who choose to obey the holy scriptures. Obeying the holy scriptures brings us into a life of temperance.

Many times the seasons of training and disciplining ourselves to have temperance, sometimes feels like a life of suffering. I like to call it, "the weeding out season." Because it seems that every contrary way within me is brought to the surface, in hopes of being purified on new dimensions. This season can often align us with clear direction and revelation regarding the kingdom of God. Based on that reward, I personally embrace those seasons of change!

4

REFLECTION PAGE:

After reading chapter 1, my reflections are:

1. _____

2. _____

3. _____

What personal commitment are you going to make regarding temperance?

1. _____

2. _____

3. _____

Areas I must repent about are:

1. _____

2. _____

3. _____

This chapter affirmed my life in the following areas:

1. _____

2. _____

3. _____

CHAPTER 2

LONG SUFFERING

Throughout this chapter we will discuss three different components of wait loss as it pertains to long suffering. Which are physical, emotional and spiritual. The ultimate goal of this chapter is to bring into focus, how we must obtain the true virtue, of what I call patience. This is a necessity during our seasons of suffering. Looking at the physical component, we hear people complaining everyday about how Hugh they have become. We look through the variety of magazines on the market today, and find so many discussions on the subject of diet. Crash diets have become the norm in many parts of our country. People are encouraged to participate in the 30-day crash diet. The hope of this plan is to rid oneself of excessive weight, by making the body suffer through deprivation, of the body's' usual food intake. I am reminded of a lady, whom I will call, Candy Bar. This lady shared a sensitive story regarding her weight loss program. The program proved to be very successful for her. However, after many months of being slim and trim, she discovered an interesting concept about herself. Her discovery was an obsession to please others. She realized that her desire for losing weight was for acceptance. After obtaining such insight about herself; Candy Bar decided that she would design a self-examination program on self-discovery. During this process, she realized that within the emotional realm of her life, that there was instability. She also discovered that her happiness was contingent upon the approval of others. This journey of self-discovery was very painful for her. Nevertheless, she decided to endure this season of self-discovery. She came to a point, where she finally accepted the truth about what others thought of her. This was beginning to sabotage her own thoughts of what her creator God thoughts were concerning her. This constant awareness of how others viewed her was quickly overshadowing Candy Bars' self-acceptance.

Then one day it was as though the green light of life came on. She then made a conscious effort to look at her real need to prioritize, what was truly important – the way others' viewed her, or the way she viewed herself through the eyes of her creator God. After many years of self-destructive suffering, it finally brought her to the journey of self-acceptance.

WHEN ONE UNDERSTANDS THE VALUE OF LONG SUFFERING, LOVE FOR ONESELF IS CAPTURED IN THE PROCESS

A very sensitive story of my childhood comes to mind, when thinking about the areas of self-acceptance. I felt very lost in the world; it seemed so big and intimidation was a constant pain within my soul. I did not know where I belonged. I started trying to figure it out at an early age. I can clearly see myself; as if it were yesterday. I am grabbing hold of my mothers' dress tail, with such fear and timidity on my face. As I reflected on the many years that brought on this timidity, much clarity was revealed to me. I then remembered the way many people had responded to me; in terms of my gender. Many times I was mistaken for being a boy. Those were the times when I had a hood over my head, and had on slacks instead of a dress. People were innocent, and meant no harm. However, I took it so personal. I am sure that I was not the only girl who went through that. I make that mistake often now, when I see a baby wearing blue. I just assume that they are a boy. My mom was always so pleasant when letting people know that I was a girl. As I got older, and became a parent, I then understood how adults can speak out of turn, and unconsciously hurt a child's feelings without realizing it. On many occasions, I have mistaken a person's daughter for a little boy. I later -apologized to the parent and their child. Unfortunately, at an early stage of my life, I had developed an inferiority complex. I felt belittled and unaccepted by others and in turn, I did not accept myself. This inferiority complex hung on to me for years. I never felt that I would be accepted as a girl. Therefore, I became, what I will call, a **tom girl.** Which, back in my days of growing up, it was really a tomboy; and that's' what I was called. Personally, I didn't feel accepted in the girlie world. For that reason, I clung to boys; and they became my best friends. The world of boys seemed safe and accepting for me. Now, what I did not know, was that there was a safer world, that I would soon encounter on life's journey. I believe that this was a set up by God.

This world, that I would soon encounter, was chosen to bring me into a life of **self-acceptance,** through a life of long-suffering. One day, while living in Buffalo, New York, during the blizzard of December 1977; I was invited to a church revival. The revival was at a loving Pentecostal church. During that time, I was sixteen years of age. My sweet Mom invited me to attend, along with some friends of hers.' At the end of the preaching portion of the revival, there was an altar call. I understood this call to mean, that it was time to accept Jesus into someone's' life. The person, who had finished preaching, encouraged everyone to come to the altar to meet Jesus. The preacher said that Jesus would deliver us from sin, which was wrong behavior before God. He also said that Jesus would **accept** a person for the way they were, and be their friend. Well, at first I rationalized my need to need Jesus. Then, after much thought, the truth of needing to be accepted is what pricked my heart. I then went to the altar. Anyways, I have always been a curious person, who would try a new thing, if given the opportunity. I then went to the altar, excited About being accepted, and gaining a new friend. To my shock, Jesus never showed up! While I was waiting, the evangelist said, **"Accept Jesus"**, and he will be your friend. At that moment, a loud shout went out over the room; people began to express happiness. I then said to myself, **"Jesus must be in the room"** Moreover, I purposed within my heart, that I would accept this altar call as a way of receiving a *new friend*; and then I would be happy, as everyone else. I remember, the evangelist preacher saying, **"come to Jesus, as you are"** this sounded great to me, because it was acceptance. Well, I accepted Jesus into my life. I then lifted my hands high, as I was instructed at the altar, by this lady, whom I will call Popcorn. I was told that, my hands lifted was considered total surrender unto the Lord Jesus. I then said these words out loud, *"Lord if you are really real as people say you are, please come into my life"* When I finished saying those words, all of a sudden, I felt happiness and a feeling of love and peace that I had never felt before. The presence felt so real until, I did not want to put my hands down, because I thought the presence would leave me.

Finally, the lady, named Popcorn, came over to me; she was so kind and loving. She then whispered these words, "baby you can sit down now, the Lord Jesus, has saved you." WOW! Those words were wonderful. I then opened my eyes, and the room looked so bright and I felt brand new. This experience was so interesting and meaningful, that I wondered if anyone else felt the same as I did. However, when I opened my eyes, there was no one standing there accept myself. Later, I pondered on the question, on whether anyone else had experienced the wonderful presence as well. Possibly you, my reader, remember such a wonderful presence. Perhaps you crave the very essence of the presence all over again. Or perhaps you've never experienced the feeling that I am talking about. Maybe your thoughts are filled with the memories of how well, it felt? Well! I have good news; you can feel that awesome presence of our Lord and Savior Jesus Christ again. The bible said that "our Lord God, will never leave us or forsake us, he will be with us until the end of the world" (Hebrews 13:5). That altar experience, to my surprise, would soon become a valuable and rewarding turning point in my life, within the area of long suffering. Several days after the experience, I was given instructions concerning the life of salvation. I was told that God had rescued me from doing bad things, and that I now had the power to control my life in a good way. In addition to that, I learned that salvation had requirements attached to it; in the areas of prayer, fasting and reading my bible. I was told, that I should pray every day, in order for me to keep closeness with God. Well, I wanted this new life; therefore, I chose to comply with all that was required of me. It all sounded okay to do. However, unbeknownst to me, I had no idea that prayer would bring me to a place, in which I would have to face up to the past issues and pains of my life. Then one day while praying, to my surprise, I began to see my childhood facing me again, I then began to cry. My tears represented, thoughts such as, "Does God really accept me as a girl?

This was a spiritual encounter that I did not know existed. Nevertheless, I left church that night feeling different. I was excited about being a Christian. Ms. Popcorn, had told me to start reading the bible. One day while studying the bible, I read these words – "wait on the Lord, and be of good courage, and he will strengthen thine heart" (Psalm 27:14). The word wait stood out amongst the rest. I only wanted to know if God had accepted me as a girl?

The wait caused me to feel a bit confused. I could not understand, at that emotional and sensitive moment, how and why the Lord would bring these biblical words to me. Being a Christian was a new and sensitive emotional time for me. I wanted to know

Gods plan for my life. The emotional side of **wait loss** seemed unbearable as well. I was of the belief that once someone accepted Jesus, these type of feelings would no longer exist. Because we put them under the **Blood of Jesus. So to speak.** I became quite disturbed at the mere fact, that the Lord had not taken away the pain of suffering, with the thought about God accepting me as a girl. I was becoming very impatient. I was losing patience. I did not want to wait for the answer. I wanted it now, right then. Also, that, the way I was answered, was with scripture verses. I desperately, wanted to know, if God had accepted me as a girl. Despite my despondency, I continued studying my bible on a daily basis. One evening, I was introduced to a new concept in my bible. This one said, "They that wait upon the Lord, shall renew their strength, they shall mount up with wings as eagles, they shall run and not be weary, they shall walk and not faint", (Isaiah 40:31). At that point I calmly asked the Lord, what is going on, and what are you trying to tell me? Here again, I waited and waited, and in the process of waiting, I became very weary. The Lord answered me not a word, What a suffering moment. Do these moments of frustration sound familiar to you my reader? As time went on, I grew to understand that the Lord did not answer me in the manner that I had hoped, because Gods ways are not my ways. I was given those times of feeling alone, because the Lord desired for me to search after righteousness, through the Holiness of Jesus. I later came to understand that God was "wooing" me into an authentic relationship. During that year, which was 1978, I was being taught the ABIDING PROCESS. All the answers that I needed, God in fact had them. However, it was more that God desired from me. Than just giving me one answered prayer. But it was more that God wanted from me, than just to give me one answered prayer. I was learning about me. My thinking was clogged with untruth that was causing ungodly pain to my emotions about who I was. I later learned that God was training me on how to filter myself out, through the abiding process.

Unfortunately, these were seeds that were planted from those who had no sense of discerning the pain and insecurity that they brought to me as a growing child. I am of the belief that children are a blank sheet of paper, and adults make their marks on them very early in their lives. Many adults never embrace the reality that children have feelings too. I am quite sure, that the adults were probably innocent; and never realized that they had hurt my feelings, about me being a boy. Yet their lack of discretion and wisdom caused a lot of pain within my soul, and it followed me into my teenage years. After spending quiet time with the Lord, I was beginning to understand its' value. I have experienced, that spending quiet moments of waiting and being still before the Lord, reveals truth about oneself. However, some people never really come to genuinely know him. The bible teaches this profound truth, "And you shall know the truth, and the truth shall make you free." (St John 8:32). Many times, truth is revealed to us, on so many levels during our times of suffering. Sometimes, the waiting period for deliverance comes very slow, and some people lose hope that God will come to their rescue. I am a firm believer that momentum should get stronger during the times of suffering. However, this only happens, if we remain faithful in Gods' word. The bible states, that the word of God is a lamp unto our feet, and a light unto our pathway. (Psalm 119:105) The Lord will order our steps, if we allow him to. Earlier, I had mentioned a very profound verse of scripture. Which said, "If you abide in me and my words abide in you, then you can ask what you will?" (St John 15:7). This scripture alone, has given me so much security. I know that God hears and will answer my prayer. I have come to understand the spirit of God, and how God moves throughout the land. It has been revealed to me through the spirit of his word. My God is very faithful, when Gods' word speaks it, then God will surely bring it to past.

We should strive very hard, not to live in denial of our emotional realm. That is the place where pain, disappointment and aguish likes to lodge and hide. Understanding this realm is vitally important. Jesus himself attempted to bring the reality of ones' emotional realm to the light. He brought comfort to the soul when he let us know, that he is in touched with what we feel. (Hebrews 4:15), He himself is touched by the feelings of our infirmities "Another way to say this, would be simply, Jesus feels what we feel, during our suffering times. That gives me great comfort. knowing that I am not alone when I suffer, Praise you Jesus! I strongly suggest getting in touch with all areas of our lives. Please stop denying that it exists. I challenge you to allow the Lord to instruct you on how to channel the emotional realm into the Spirit. I know, this area is untapped, when it comes to Christendom. Our God is faithful with helping us to become free agents of intimacy with him. Have you ever heard the phrase, *my emotions deceived me*, this phrase has proven to be true within my personal life? Emotional feelings are one of the senses that God created when we were brought into existence. However, it is important that we direct them through the proper channels. The channel, that I recommend is prayer. Throughout life we encounter strong feelings about certain situations. Often times, our emotions will take us on a journey of long suffering, this can be very painful. Here is a personal and dear story that means a lot to me. During the year of 1992, my beautiful mother died, and went home to be with the Lord. Two weeks prior to my Mothers' passing, I had birthed my third adorable child, her name is Tonya Marie. My mothers' passing was very sad on one level of my emotions. On another level, I was over joyed that she made it into the kingdom of heaven; I knew that was what she wanted. After several months had passed, I found that one level of my emotions began to wonder if she had in fact gone home to be with the Lord, for real. Or if she was still here, and her death was faked. This emotional thought brought, stress and anxiety to my entire being. As a result, I had sleepless nights, very painful headaches, and many times my life felt as though it was literally leaving my body. I then decided to see my Doctor. The report from her was that, I was possibly in a state of denial. This denial was the result of me having panic attacks, frustration and anxiety. Personally, I did not like this diagnosis.

The doctor prescribed a medicine; and told me to see her within 6months. After leaving her office, I decided not to take the prescription. I then put together a spiritual Plan for my life that would bring comfort, life and healing to my body, in the emotional realm in hopes of reviving me and putting me back on track. One of the spiritual prescriptions that sustained me during that time of emotional suffering was; 1st Peter 5:7. For approximately six months, I directed my emotions to a level of prayer and meditation. After six months, I went back to my Doctor; she gave me a complete checkup, and said that I was doing fine. Silence then filled the room. The Doctor asked me, what did I do? I let her know that I took the bible as the final authority for my healing. In the case of dealing with the loss of my mother, it was prayer that restored my emotional stability, and regained the courage and strength to wait upon God, with TOTAL FAITH.

REFLECTION PAGE

After reading Chapter 2, my reflections area:

1. _____

2. _____

3. _____

I will make a personal commitment to:

1. _____

2. _____

3. _____

Areas I must repent about are:

1. _____

2. _____

3. _____

This chapter affirmed my life in the following areas:

1. _____

2. _____

3. _____

CHAPTER 3

SEEDS OF FAITH

Our next journey is a faith filled day. Each day we should discipline ourselves to believe God throughout the entire day. From my very own experience, I know that God is faithful. Seeing that God is faithful, it is required of the believer to have faith in God only. The bible wrote, "Now, faith is the substance of things hoped for, and the evidence of things not seen" (Hebrews 11:1). Faith is seen in the Spirit, the place where we communicate with God. Let us remember, that God is a Spirit, and we must worship him in spirit and in truth. What you are believing God to do for you must already be seen through the eyes of faith. It is vitally important, for us to do away with all doubt and disbelief. Hebrews 11:6 says "He who comes to God must believe that he is and that he is a rewarder of those who diligently seek him". The manifestation is already here, once we believe, and train our vision to be crystal clear from the eyes of the Spirit. The bible said "to call those things that be not as though they were", (Romans 4:17). This scripture is vital for us to remember because there is so much around us that can cause us to lose our focus of faith. However, as we train ourselves to see situations through the word of God, our bible, then our faith increases. I can recall moments in my life, when I was taught at church, that it was okay to lay your hands on what you wanted and then claim it for yourself. That teaching provoked me and others to lay my hands on cars, clothes, and whatever else that I desired to be blessed with from God. Many times, that point of faith did in fact bring those blessings into my life. However, those blessings came with much debt, and struggle. The bible says, "The blessings of the Lord makes rich and adds no sorrow, (Proverbs 10:22).

As I have grown into the knowledge of God, on new levels in God; I now understand that there are seasons for certain blessings. Because, of my lack of understanding many hasty decisions were made. I now, teach my children, about the importance of not being hasty. Having faith, and being hasty, is truly a bad mixture.

As you plant seeds of faith, you are cultivating your faith on new dimensions each day. Eventually, you will see the fruit of your labor, is manifested. I like to tell people to position themselves for the blessing. For example, when you plant flower seeds, you do not see the pretty flowers the same day. However, each day when you water those seeds and provide ample sunlight, you are cultivating the growth of the flower... Our lives are that flower, and it works the same way. As we read our bible, pray, and speak the word of God into every situation, our faith grows in God. There is seed time, and harvest. When your season of blessings come, there will be no sorrow, only riches and wealth; contingent upon the seeds that you have sown. The bible says, "The crown of the wise is their riches" (Proverbs 14:24). I am a firm believer that what God has for you, is yours, and will be given to you at the right and appointed time. People will see your riches, in every area of your life; because you were wise enough to plant seeds of faith and to cultivate them. Let me caution you, my friend; please don't be hasty and impatient. "Trust in the Lord with all thine heart, and lean not to your own understanding, acknowledge God in all your ways, and he shall direct your path" (Proverbs 5:6). Allowing God to direct your path is an act of your faith. Keep in mind, that God knows what is best for you. The bible says, be not wise in thine own eyes, (Proverbs 3:7). Perhaps, it is time for you my reader to cultivate your faith to another dimension. How about exploring new dimensions and areas with God. For example, if you know that God told you to go back to school and educate yourself; then do it by faith. Please do not look at circumstances. I encourage you to go online, get information about the school, and prepare yourself to register for classes. That process is what cultivates your faith, so go for it! I love this verse of scripture, "FAITH COMETH BY HEARING THE WORD OF GOD", (Romans 10:17). It is your choice, my reader.

CULTIVATING YOUR FAITH IS TOTALLY UP TO YOU!

I encourage you to desire true and lasting faith, which is established through the word of God. David the psalmist said, "The word is a lamp unto my feet, and a light unto my pathway" (Psalm 119:105). In addition to hearing the word of God, we also must speak what the bibles said... Here is a quote, that I once heard, "you can't move a mountain with dirt in your mouth." What this quote is saying is, that a mouth filled with unbelief, fear, doubt and anxiety, is not faith talk. Faith talk is speaking Gods word back to him. He said in the bible, to "bring him into remembrance of his word" (Isaiah 43:26). I believe that God wants us to bring him into remembrance, as a way for us to remember; I call that reverse psychology. Remember, God is God, and he does not forget his words. Also remember, that our "God is able to do exceedingly abundantly, above all that we ask or even think" (Ephesians 3:20). The power in that verse is referring to *faith in God's word, the bible.* Our faith in God is the ultimate. He is so faithful. If God said it, he then will be sure that it happens. According to the scriptures, our God is not a man that he would lie. If God's word states something, you can rest assure that it is

ETCHED IN STONE, so to speak. God's word is sure. When we begin to take his word as the truth of our faith, we will experience progress in our lives, on new dimensions. Also when others see your faith, then others are affected by your decision of faith. The bible said to let your light so shine before others that they may see your GOOD WORKS, and glorify your father which is in heaven. Having faith in God is quite a challenge because you do not see God with your physical eye, but you know he is present by what you feel and see him doing within your life. Faith is a challenge of your belief system. If you do not believe God, then you will show it by what you don't do. Let's pause for a moment. I want to walk a journey of reflection with you right now. This journey of reflection is designed to challenge you to look at the areas of your life, where faith has been diluted by what I call…hidden tumors.

Perhaps you can envision those moments when the following tumors began to grow within you; such as anger, feelings of defeat, loss, regret, shame, doubt, or a pool of self-pity. Now, while reading this book, you are beginning to understand that these areas were able to oppress your life because you had stopped believing God, and trusting the biblical truths of the bible. I sense a prompting within my spirit, to tell you, that you can start your restoration process at this very moment. God wants to restore your total faith in him, and him alone. I once read in my bible, that we the believer, are to have faith in God! However, in order for you to be restored, there Is an important role that you must play. Are you ready? Well, let's start, one, two, three, let's go…, First you must become your own personal surgeon, and be willing to examine your areas of where there has been a lack of faith in God. Secondly, those areas must be brought under the surgeon's microscopic lens, to find out how contaminated you have become; and how big those areas of a lack of faith have grown. By giving these areas a complete examination, you will discover, a clear understanding, regarding, the angle that you should start your attack of removing those vicious, and subtle tumors. Your concentration and focus, must be a daily, second by second attack. It is vitally important for your attack towards these areas to be gently handled; yet no longer tolerated. YOU! The surgeon must not leave any piece of its existence. This surgery can be as successful, as you want it to be; it's up to you, my reader. The old saying is *"HOW BAD DO YOU WANT IT?"*

Let me caution you, my friend, that money cannot pay for this surgery. It is important that you recognize the length of time that this tumor has affected the progress of your dreams. My final instruction is for you to repent, because you allowed things and behaviors, contrary to God's plan for your life to dominate, and consume your faith in God alone. Now, at this moment, take authority over every spirit that is not of God, and command it to leave your life. Command your FAITH in God to come alive again. The bible says, "Now FAITH IS THE SUBSTANCE OF THINGS HOPED, AND THE EVIDENCE OF THINGS NOT SEEN", (Hebrews 11:1). When we are admonished to have faith in God; we should move into the frame of thought immediately, before contemplation sets in. We should take on an attitude of pleasing only God. The bible says, "Without faith, it is impossible to please God." (Hebrews 11:6). When I personally think about having faith in God, my mind and vision goes towards my favorite bird, which is the eagle. I love to see eagles in pictures, books, jewelry, and statues; they are my favorite collections. I love being in the presence of an eagle. The eagle is steady, has tenacity, and it moves in a realm of faith. Remember that God made the eagle. Therefore, I am convinced that only God put a personality of tenacity within the precious bird. Eagles, never allow the storms of life to keep them from flying. Storms provoke them to only fly higher; they are my best friends. When I meet people who do not linger on the storms of life, I really enjoy being around them.

Those people represent eagles, and I gain strength and enjoyment when I am in their presenceThe eagles faith, keeps them from being distracted. They will lock their wings, and just fly higher; they have tunnel vision, so to speak. Hey, question; are you an eagle, do you have eagle's wings? Just wondering. A true eagle waits upon God, that is so cool to me!, even when they are feeling weak in the faith, they are persuaded, that their God is faithful, and that their strength will someday be renewed. Look at what the prophet Isaiah, had to say about eagles: "they that wait upon the Lord, shall renew their strength, they shall mount up with wings as eagles, they shall run and not be weary; they shall walk and not faint" (Isaiah 40:31). I encourage, you my reader, to keep the faith of God, and watch the goodness of our sweet Jesus comfort you.

REFLECTION PAGE:

After reading Chapter 3, my reflections are:

1. _____

2. _____

3. _____

What personal commitment are you going to make regarding Faith?

1. _____

2. _____

3. _____

Areas I must repent about are:

1. _____

2. _____

3. _____

This chapter affirmed my life in the following areas:

1. _____

2. _____

3. _____

CHAPTER 4

GOODNESS

This chapter is about the goodness of God. The bible states that, "the goodness of God leads to repentance, (Romans 2:4). When we accept, and understand how good God really is, our lives will become happy. Our God really loves us, and does care about us. As we receive this within our hearts, it will provoke us to live with a heart of repentance. I believe that many times people live with guilt and shame, because they have not taken the time to search out God's goodness. The bible says "Taste and see that the Lord is good (Psalm 34:8). Many times we have wanted people to be good to us. However, on many levels, their goodness comes with so many conditions. The love of God is unconditional. You do not have to jump through hoops, so to speak", to have consistent love from God. You can truly trust him; "yeah that's what' s up!", as my dear husband Maurice would often say. Our God is good, therefore his love is freely given, without any strings attached. The bible admonishes the saints, (the people of God's kingdom), to rejoice in goodness, as a child of the kingdom (2 Chronicles 6:14). It has to be an act of our will, choosing to rejoice in goodness. This subject of goodness is so great, because, our bible says that it follows us all the days of our lives (Psalm 23:6), and knowing this should be enough to make us rejoice. There are many negative circumstances surrounding us each day; my response to that is, SO WHAT! OUR God is faithful. We should always live in expectation of our Gods glory and awesome presence. We see the pain and distress of drive by shootings, gang violence, divorce, deceit, and this evil list can go on and on. Despite the negative reports, let us train ourselves, to get excited about happy marriages, happy children, good success, unity, drive by prayer and gift giving and this list can go on and on as well. You see, my reader, it is your own free will, as to accept an evil report, or to see a GOOD REPORT. It's all a matter of perspective. For example,

I read the story of Joshua, Caleb, and the spies. They were all sent up by God, to spy out a particular land. When they came back to give the report, some focused on the giants in the land. However, Joshua and Caleb focused on conquering the giants. They did not let the negative perspective over take their eyes of victory. My question to you my reader is what do you see? David the Psalmist said "I had fainted, unless I had believed to see the goodness of the Lord in the land of the living" (Psalm 27:13). As we watch the news, read newspapers and engage in conversations, we hear about people who have given up on life. Many areas have defeated them such as, suicide, abuse, depression, loneliness, hopelessness, and many sorts of guilt and shame. However, when we take a moment to reflect upon the GOODNESS of Jesus, it brings a ray of hope and rejoicing into our lives. Psalm 31:19, reads; "Oh how great is thy goodness, which thou have laid up for them that fear thee." As we look around us, our Gods GOODNESS is prevalent throughout the land. The bible says, "The earth is full of the goodness of the Lord" (Psalm 33:5). God's goodness is continuous (Psalm 52:1). There is no end to Gods' GOODNESS. There are no time constraints to Gods' display of goodness. Lets' just learn to praise our fantastic God. It feels so good to me when

I take a praise break; focusing on the goodness of God and his unfailing love for me. Try taking a praise break right now, you will be happy that you did, *enjoy*! Learning to praise God for his goodness brings peace and comfort, I have experienced this. Meditate on this for a moment... "Oh *that men would praise the lord for his goodness, and his wonderful works, towards the children of men.*" (Psalm 107:8). If we would discipline ourselves to praise God, our lives will be fulfilled on a daily basis. Now, meditate on these words... "For *he satisfied the longing soul and filleth the hungry soul with goodness.*" (*Psalm* 107:9).

Please, always remember that the Lord is good to all. The Lord Gods' tender mercies are over all his works. God blesses the just and the unjust. His goodness motivates him to bless you. Check this out, Matthew 5:45. Gods *GOODNESS* is wrapped up in one fruit basket. "For *the fruit of the Spirit is in all* GOODNESS" (*Ephesians* 5:9). All that we need or want is given to us, because our God is simply just Good.

We pray always for you, that our God would count you worthy of his calling and fulfill all the good pleasure of his goodness," (2ⁿᵈ Thessalonians 1:11), and always remember these words. Gods' goodness is only a sign of his true love for each one of us. (St. John 3: 16).

REFLECTION PAGE:

After reading Chapter 4, my reflections are:

1. _____

2. _____

3. _____

I will make a personal commitment to:

1. _____

2. _____

3. _____

Areas that I must repent about are:

1. _____

2. _____

3. _____

This chapter affirmed my life in the following areas:

1. _____

2. _____

3. _____

CHAPTER 5

LOVE

This chapter is about the love of God, which reminds me of the Prego Spaghetti Sauce commercial. This commercial was out during the 80's. The advertisers, put it this way, "It's in there" that spaghetti sauce was known as being the best; because of the hidden ingredients that went into making it tasty and spicy. We didn't have to add any other ingredients to make it tastier, it was already perfect. All that was asked of us is that we purchase the product, open the jar, and pour the sauce into a pan, heat it up and stir. After that process was finished, we then poured the sauce over the spaghetti, put it on the table and ate. When the family are all gathered at the table, they are then drawn to this perfect meal. No one had to add salt or pepper because it's all in there. The family impatiently waited for the table grace to be said, because they were ready to dig in. This is the same with our Lord God, it's all in there. All that we need and want is in the love of God, through Jesus Christ. Jesus has been the perfect ingredient, chosen by God, to give us the spice for life. That spice of life is his LOVE. He unselfishly died on the cross of Calvary to give us life. The bible says, "For God so loved the world, that he gave his only begotten son, that whosoever believeth on him, should not perish, but shall have everlasting life" (St. John 3:16). David the Psalmist revealed the love of God, when he shared the profound truth about us being wonderfully made (Psalm 139:14). God loves us so much, that he took the time to make us with wonder. This alone provokes me to stand in awe and reverence of him. Paul the apostle, shared the amazing story of the inner workings of God, that is within all of us, (Philippians 2:13). God's love comes to cover our hearts. The bible says, that the love of God is shed abroad in our hearts, by the Holy Ghost, which is given unto us, (Romans 5:5). Also the Love, of God constrains us (2nd Corinthians 5:14). I have experienced this within my own personal life

Lets' look at one of my favorite bible illustration of Gods' inner workings. People enjoy judging our lives based on what they see, but our God looks at our hearts, yeah! In the book of 1st Samuel 16:7, we hear the story about Jesse's sons. The Lord was ready for a new king. God sent Samuel to choose one from among the house of Jesse. He showed Samuel all of his sons, except for one. However, Samuel did not have the peace of God, about choosing one of the sons. He then asked him if he had anymore sons. Jesse hesitantly said yes; he then brought David to Samuel. The Lord then put a check within Samuels's heart, that David would be the chosen king

I truly believe that God chooses positions for his people, based on the position of the love of God within our hearts. The bible tells us to love the Lord with all of our heart, (Deuteronomy 30: 6). Before we can truly love God with all of our hearts, we must understand what the love of God really is. Open your bible and turn to 1st Corinthians chapter 13. This is the love chapter that puts everything back into perspective. **Love suffers long**, and many times we want to give up on people, when they act in ways that we do not like. However, the love of God causes us to be patient and to endure the struggling times with them. **Love is kind,** this means to have a sympathetic attitude towards others. **Love envieth not,** this means to be happy for others, and not covetous of what they have. **Love vaunted not itself;** this is when you promote your own glory, to lift yourself higher. **Love does not behave unseemly,** doing those things in which we know are contrary to the word of God. **Love seeketh not your own, meaning unselfishness.** This means to look out for the benefit of others. **Love is not easily provoked;** this simply means that you are not quick to allow someone else's' point of view to disturb your peace. **Love thinketh no evil,** perhaps, this is the toughest of all. Nevertheless, we are admonished to think the very best about all people and circumstances always. **Love rejoiced not in iniquity.** We are not to be happy when people are entertaining sin.

We should pray for them. **Love rejoiced in the truth,** this means that we are happy for others when they see the light of righteousness... **Love beareth all things,** this means to endure difficult and painful times together, because it is only temporary. **Love believeth all things,** this means to have total trust in God. **Love hoped all things,** always seeing the best in every situation. **Love endured all things,** this mean to support a situation indefinitely.

To you my reader, we have both learned about unconditional love. I believe, if we would discipline ourselves to meditate upon the love scriptures on a daily basis, then there would be less turmoil within our homes, churches, schools, and our community at large. I believe that there would be many more people coming into the body of Jesus Christ. The Lord Jesus said, "With love and kindness have I drawn you." (Jeremiah 31; 3) A sure sign that we love God, is when we keep his commandments, (St. John 14:15). God admonishes us throughout the bible to put on righteous character and attributes, that represent the kingdom of God. We are told "not to love in word only, but indeed and in truth," (1st John 3:18). We can tell people throughout the day that we love them. However, it is only lip service if it is not genuinely from the heart. It must come from the truth of our hearts. The love of God is a journey with many levels of adapting to his ways. People know that we love God, by the way that we treat them. Meditate on this scripture; 'whoso has this worlds goods and seeth his brother has need, and shutteth up his bowels of compassion from him, how dwelleth the love of God in him", (1ˢᵗ John 3:17). The love of God is vital. It helps us to comprehend and understand all saints. I love this profound scripture, check this out; "That he would grant you, according to the riches of his glory, to be strengthened with might, by his spirit in the inner man, that Christ may dwell in your hearts by faith that ye, being rooted and grounded in love, may be able to comprehend with all saints, what is the breath and length, and depth, and height" (Ephesians 3:16-18).

The love of God should be the ultimate authority in the Christians life. We can display many Christian gestures. However, without love, our existence is useless. The bible closes out the love chapter, as such; "Though we speak with the tongues of men, and of angels, and have not love, we are considered sounding brass, or a tinkling cymbal, and though we have the gift of prophecy, and understand all mysteries, and all knowledge and though we have all faith, so that we can move mountains, and have not charity, we are nothing, and though we bestow all our goods to feed the poor and though we give our body to be burned and have not charity it profited us nothing" (1ˢᵗ Corinthians 13: 1-3). Let us accept the love of God, for truly that is a display of gentleness.

REFELECTION PAGE

After reading chapter 5, my reflections are:

1. _____

2. _____

3. _____

I will make a personal commitment to:

1. _____

2. _____

3. _____

Areas that I must repent about are:

1. _____

2. _____

3. _____

This chapter affirmed my life, in the following areas:

1. _____

2. _____

3. _____

CHAPTER 6

GENTLENESS

The bible tells us to be gentle unto all people, (2ⁿᵈ Timothy 2:24). We are admonished not to be brawlers. Meaning noisy and quarrelsome; but we are to be *gentle*, showing all meekness unto all men, (Titus 3:2). The bible speaks about gentleness, being wisdom. The wisdom that is from above is first pure, then peaceable, *gentle* and easy to be entreated, (James 3:17). God's gentleness brings greatness to all of the saints, as we allow it to become an attribute into our lives. Read, 2ⁿᵈ Samuel 22:36 which said, "Thou hast also given me the shield of thy salvation, and thy gentleness hast made me great." In this verse David the Psalmist chose to allow God's gentleness to possess his life. He decided to walk in the way of gentleness, displaying a mild temper. The rewards for a life filled with gentleness is great. During the times of testing and trials, we are tempted to fall into an attitude of anger and disappointment. However, when we allow our minds to be engulfed with gentleness, we then will become very calm in the situation. It is important to train ourselves on how to approach people in a way that displays gentleness. This attribute is displayed also in the life of Christ, (2ⁿᵈ Corinthians 10:1). "Now I Paul, I beseech you by the gentleness of Christ". As we allow ourselves to take on a life of gentleness, I believe that God will be pleased. It is important for the benefit of the kingdom of God that others see and feel the gentleness of Jesus Christ within our lives. Keep in mind that so many people are mistreated and mishandled so harshly. When a Christian comes into the room, it should be refreshing for them because Christians should exuberant the love and peace of God with gentleness. I have often thought about the woman with the issue of blood, whose story is in the bible. I believe that, she gently touched the helm of Jesus' garment. His response was, "who touched me" (Luke chapter 1). Being gentle demonstrates our trust in God. Believing that God has everything under control. Learn to trust God! There is a verse of scripture that states, our God shall repay, (Romans 12:19). Even when people choose to be our enemies, we never have to allow ourselves to become vindictive.

Personally, I believe that the Lord gave us this verse of scripture to keep us grounded. If we know that vengeance belongs to God and he will repay, then all we have to do is trust. I have come to understand this verse as a way of helping me to keep myself kind and gentle and to keep me from dealing with a negative situation in a dirty and messy way. It is up to the Christian believer to cultivate the attributes of gentleness. Steps to cultivate gentleness are: First, we must recognize the need for gentleness. Secondly, we must learn all of the biblical scriptures concerning gentleness. Thirdly, we must meditate on the scriptures daily. The bible said to meditate upon the word day and night then we will be like a tree planted by the rivers of water, (Psalm chapter 1). As we work through the abiding process to cultivate a gentle disposition, we will become more like Jesus. The bible said, "If ye abide in me and my words abide in you, we can ask what we will and it shall be done unto us" (St. John 15:7). The gentleness comes as we abide consciously in Gods' presence. Let's look at the widow in the bible, (Luke 18:1-8).

She had many petitions which she brought to the unjust judge. This man was very stubborn and did not want to honor her petitions. Nevertheless, she continued going to him. Finally, he decided to give her what she wanted. She was determined to weary him until her request was honored. I believe that her gentle spirit and disposition broke the hardness of his heart. We as Christians have been given the power and authority to break wickedness. I want to encourage you to ask God, to help you to be a gentle Christian. Our God is present to help us. He is a very present help in the time of trouble, (Psalm 46:1). We can truly look out to the hills from whence cometh our help, it comes from the Lord (Psalm 121). Our Lord God tells us to call upon him, because he wants to do great and mighty things in our lives, (Jeremiah 33:3).

Let us always remember that, gentleness is an attribute that we must possess with joy.

REFLECTION PAGE

After reading Chapter 6, my reflections are:

1. _____

2. _____

3. _____

I will make a personal commitment to:

1. _____

2. _____

3. _____

Areas that I must repent about are:

1. _____

2. _____

3. _____

This chapter affirmed my life in the following areas:

1. _____

2. _____

3. _____

CHAPTER 7

JOY

M any times we go through life asking God to strengthen us, when in actuality we need to be petitioning him for JOY. Gods' joy is the strength and enduring power that is readily available to us. I read the story about Nehemiah 8:10. Ezra assisted Nehemiah with accomplishing the goal of reviving the people of Israel. Bringing spiritual recovery and commitment back to the people through Gods' word. The people had many hardships along their journey and were very weary. Their only hope of recovery was recommitment to God. They tried finding their own strength. However, that did not work. Ezra, then had to let them know that what, they needed was the JOY of the Lord. In other words, they needed their excitement for God restored. That excitement for God would become their strength for enduring hard times. How many times have you tried coping with the cares of this life, by your own strength? For a while, you may have felt good and in total control. However, it later fell through. Suddenly, you realized that you had put God out of the equation. The reality of needing Gods help was evident. Let me beg of you, my reader; please abide in God, through Jesus Christ. From my experience, the following biblical words can be your stability, if you like. "If you abide in me, and my words abide in you, then you can ask for what you will and it shall be done unto you". The children of Israel were out of sync with God and had to realign themselves again. This time they had to realign themselves with an understanding that their strength would only be in their joy for the Lord. Habakkuk, pinned it down when he said, "Yet I will rejoice in the Lord, I will JOY in the God of my salvation" (Habakkuk 3:18). He was undergoing some difficult challenges. He acknowledged where his joy would come from. There will be times in our lives, when we do not feel the presence of joy. We can then ask God to restore the joy. Also, to couple that joy with feelings of euphoria. David the Psalmist, wrote "Thou wilt show me the path of life. In thy presence is fullness of joy". At thy right hand are pleasures for evermore, (Psalm 16:11). My personal experience with the joy of the Lord has been evident strength during time of despair. In November of the year 2012, I got divorced after being married for twenty-five years. My emotions felt so much pain and despair. I felt very disappointed, lost and empty. I had married at a very early time of my life. I loved my family of five. They were my rock of stability. Here I was now alone. My children had all completed college. They were discovering Gods plan for their own lives. I was now home alone with my two dogs, Princess and Punch.

Each day I sat quietly in my prayer room, asking the Holy Spirit to comfort and guide me. I never wanted to do life without my husband. Each day my inner drive was becoming weak. I was losing many levels of drive and inspiration. The feeling of humiliation and abandonment felt unbearable. The thought of having a different name from my children was very hard. We were all Coplin' legally. I did not want people to think that I had my children out of wedlock.

We were a Christian family with an established ministry in the community. Also ordained clergy, as Ministers and Pastors. I asked God to show me how to be strong for my three wonderful children. While studying my bible, one day I remembered the scripture that said; "The joy of the Lord is your strength" (Nehemiah 8:10). This scripture became my daily meditation. Each day the sheer joy of Gods' joy penetrated my emotion of pain and despair.

I started feeling new energy and vitality. I was not only smiling on the outside now, but I had an inner smile as well. God quickly gave me emotional health, and renewed strength to live. My next big step was forgiveness. Each day I started voicing the confession. "I forgive, I forgive, I forgive, because I want to live "I desperately wanted to survive this painful season of my life. I wanted to have the testimony of Gods' redeeming love and joy. The Lord helped me to survive that season. I stayed steadfast and unmovable, abounding in the work of the Lord. I did not compromise with anyone or anything out of the parameters of God. I stayed faithful to my commitment to holiness. After that season a year later, God allowed me to see a classmate at FedEx Kinko's. We had not seen each other in over 33 years. He came inside FedEx Kinko's with a walker, and a back brace. He looked tore up, from the floor up, so to speak. When he spoke to the salesman, I then said to him, I know that voice. I told him that I knew him from somewhere. When I looked at his eyes, they looked familiar as well. He did not remember me. He was in recovery from Plasmocytoma Cancer. He had experienced a lot of memory lost from undergoing chemotherapy, radiation and being in a coma for over thirty days.

He then said to me, did you go to Riverside High School? I said yes. He then said are you Tee. I said yes. He then asked for my phone number. He asked if he could call me sometimes. I said yes. For some strange reason, I was quickened in my heart to say to him, I am the last dot in your life. I had no idea, why those words came to me that I blurted out of my mouth to him.

Well, we met up at the park one evening. He asked if I would help him to walk again. I was excited about helping my high school classmate. I was thankful to the Lord for giving me a mission. This would help me to keep my mind on something productive and evangelistic. I was determined to keep myself Holy before the Lord. I did not want to date. Deep down inside I was hoping that my husband would ask me to reconcile with him and restore our family. While waiting for that to happen, I purposed in my heart to be whole heartedly present for my classmate. He needed me and I did not want to let him down. David the Psalmist said these words, (Psalm 51:12)," Restore unto me the JOY of thy salvation." I know that there will be times when you do not feel joy and will feel weary. From my own experience, I know that our Lord God will restore it back to you, just ask believing it so. Our bible lets' us know, if we believe something when we pray, that God will grant it unto us, if we don't doubt. As we choose to abide in Jesus Christ, our God shows us the path of life. David said, "Thou wilt show me the path of life; in thy presence is fullness of joy; at thy right hand, are pleasures for evermore" (Psalm 16:11). With Gods' joy we can draw out of the wells of salvation, (Isaiah 12:3). That is powerful! Wells of salvation are a deep source of energy. I love the word of God, as it referred to JOY, I love what Jeremiah said, "Thy word was unto me, the joy and rejoicing of mine heart", (Jeremiah 15:16). Sometimes when we are facing our enemy, it can be hard and difficult for us to lift up our heads and show courage and strength. Nevertheless, David the Psalmist put it this way. "And now shall my head be lifted up above my enemies, round about me; therefore, will I offer in his tabernacle sacrifices of joy" (Psalm 27:6). Gods' word should be received with JOY. Let's look at an account in the book of Luke, chapter 8. Those by the wayside are they that hear the word, which is the bible, then the devil cometh and taketh away the word out of their hearts. Lest they should believe and be saved, those on the rock are they which when they hear, receive the word with joy. According to St. Luke 10:17, it says the following, "The seventy returned again with joy, saying Lord, even the devils are subject unto us through thy name." Jesus has commanded us to keep his commandments, we have been admonished to do that, so that our joy might be full, (St. John 15:10-11). Jesus has promised to turn our sorrows into joy. "Verily, verily, I say unto you, that ye shall weep and lament, but the world shall rejoice and ye shall be sorrowful, but your sorrow shall be turned into joy" (St. John 16:20). Please know, that during your season of life's challenges, you do not have to turn to evil things. Our God is faithful. In the book of Psalm – 84:11. It states, "no good thing will God withhold from those who walk upright." Often times during painful seasons, somethings are so unjust. We cry and long for the season to come to a halt. Crying is a normal catharsis. Please never give up on righteousness. In the midst of your tears, there is a flow of joy coming your way. The bible references this profound, and rich scripture. "They that sow in tears, shall reap in joy, (Psalm 126:5). I love this scripture so much. The more that I meditate on this scripture, I am even more inspired to keeping myself humble and meek before the Lord.

Joy can be used to empower others with the joy of God. Let us look at Paul and Barnabas. "When therefore Paul and Barnabas had no small dissension and disputation with them, they determined that Paul, Barnabas and certain others of them should go up to Jerusalem unto the apostles and elders about this question, and being brought on their way by the church they passed through Phoenicia and Samaria, declaring the conversion of the gentiles; and they caused great joy unto all the brethren" (Acts 15:2-3). Jesus is our example, in terms of a focus of joy. "Looking unto Jesus, the author and finisher of our faith, who for the joy that was set before him endured the cross, despising the shame, is set down at the right hand of the throne of God" (Hebrews 12:2). Often times, when we are enduring our seemingly cross experience, we may cry and shed many tears of sorrow. To you my reader, do not give up! In the midst of your tears, JOY is on the way! The bible said, "They that sow in tears, shall reap in joy" (Psalm 126:5). Also, people will know that you are living with the joy of the Lord, by the way you answer to situations around you. "A man hath joy, by the answer of his mouth" (Proverbs 15:23). Our God is faithful. The Lord blessed me to get married again. My high school classmate and I reconnected after 33 years. We established a beautiful friendship. After dating for 3 and a half years. He asked me to marry him. The rest is history. To God be the glory !

ABIDE IN GODS' PRESENCE, AND WATCH GODS' JOY UNFOLD IN YOUR LIFE, AONG WITH MEEKNESS

REFLECTION PAGE

After reading Chapter 7, my reflections are:

1. _____

2. _____

3. _____

I will make a personal commitment to:

1. _____

2. _____

3. _____

Areas I must repent about are:

1. _____

2. _____

3. _____

This chapter affirmed my life in the following areas:

1. _____

2. _____

3. _____

CHAPTER 8

MEEKNESS

According to the bible, "blessed are the meek, for they shall inherit the earth", (Matthew 5:5). I am a firm believer that meekness must be cultivated. It is the believer's responsibility to study the word of God and to meditate on scriptures that inspire and motivate us towards a life style of meekness.

For us to inherit the earth, we must learn the value of meekness. It should be something that we hold in high esteem. Meekness is simply a life of humility and submission unto God. The bible says "by humility and the fear of the Lord, are riches, honor and life", (Proverbs 22: 4). Meekness is what we should present to people when they have been overtaken in some kind of fault.

According to the bible, "Brethren, if a man be overtaken in a fault ye which are spiritual, restore such a one in the spirit of meekness, considering thyself lest thou also be tempted", (Galatians 6:1). It is our responsibility to care enough for people. that we lead them towards restoration. This attitude pleases God. It is extremely important for us to present an attitude of meekness.

The bible says, "but thou oh man, of God flee these things, and follow after righteousness, godliness, faith, love, patience and meekness, (1st Timothy 6:11). We are instructed through the Holy Scriptures, that we should never speak evil of anyone, according to Titus 3:2, which said, "To speak evil of no man, to be no brawlers, but gentle showing all meekness unto all men". Wow! Just think how honorable that would be in the sight of God. We are to receive the word of God with meekness. The bible says to "Lay apart all filthiness and superfluity of naughtiness and receive with meekness the engrafted word, which is able to save your souls", (James 1:21).

Our souls must demonstrate wisdom through a lifestyle of meekness. "Who is a wise man and endued with knowledge among you, let him show out of a good conversation, his works with meekness of wisdom", (James 3:13). Our conversations should demonstrate the sanctity of God within our hearts. We are admonished to sanctify God in our hearts for the benefit of those around us.

"But sanctify the Lord God in your hearts and be ready always to give an answer to every man that asketh you a reason of the hope that is in you with meekness and fear", (1st Peter 3:15). Ladies and Gentlemen, our God is calling us into a deeper focus to the biblical direction concerning meekness. Jesus was meek and lowly in heart, (Matthew 11:29).

Jesus is our role model and what was required of him in character, is truly required of the Christian believer as well. I know there will be times when you get very frustrated with yourself because you are not measuring up to the standards of the bible. It may even seem easier to compromise with the standards and expectations of the worldly pleasures. Nevertheless, Jesus has shown us how to overcome the world.

Jesus told us how he overcame the world. Jesus said "be of good cheer for I have overcome the world", (St. John 16:33). I believe that throughout each challenge of our lives, that it is pertinent for us to develop an attitude of meekness. Jesus, our humble example, was able to endure the sins and cares of the world, because he was seeing through the eyes of faith and obedience unto God. Jesus was filled with the joy of doing all things unto Father God and not for his selfish glory and recognition.

"Who for the joy, that was set before him, he endured the cross, despising the shame", (Hebrews 12:22). I love Jesus so much and each day I am so thankful that I have accepted him as Lord of my life. He knew and understood the power and benefits of meekness. Let us begin to discipline ourselves today and learn of the meekness of Jesus and apply his teachings of love, unity, respect for self and for others, etc. now!

It is time to inherit the earth and bring the necessary changes. "Blessed are the meek, for they shall inherit the earth", (Matthew 5:5). There is so much peace that comes with having a life of MEEKNESS. This is a known fact from my own personal experiences in life. When I humble myself and open my heart to obey and love the holy scriptures, it is a sure sign that I am trusting Gods direction for my life.

Let's close this chapter with the following scripture verse, "Great Peace have they, which love thy law, and nothing shall offend them," (Psalm 119:165). I enjoy God's peace...IT'S PRICELESS!

REFLECTION PAGE

After reading chapter 8, my reflections are:

1. _____

2. _____

3. _____

I will make a personal commitment to:

1. _____

2. _____

3. _____

Areas, I must repent about are:

1. _____

2. _____

3. _____

This chapter affirmed, my life in the following areas:

1. _____

2. _____

3. _____

CHAPTER 9

PEACE

According to the Biblical Scriptures our God has ordained peace for you! The bible says, "Great peace have they who love they law and nothing shall offend them", (Psalm 119:165). I believe that it is vitally important that we acknowledge the value of loving God's word, the bible. Many of us have taken an offence to the way some people treat Christian believers. Despite the ill treatment, we are still admonished in the scriptures as to how we should respond. Overcoming evil with good is supposed to be the Christians' response. The bible of our Holy God is our defense. Exodus Chapter 14:14 says, the Lord shall fight for you and you shall hold your peace." I love the word peace. The key word in that verse is **hold.** when I hear that word my mind and heart begins to take on calmness. Peace means freedom from anxiety, annoyance, mental and emotional unrest.

The Lord told his servant Job these words, "hearken unto me, hold thy peace and I shall teach thee wisdom." (Job 33:33) Many situations will come to disturb our peace but we must fight spiritually to hold on to our peace... don't let it go! While holding on to our peace and waiting on Gods' leading through the Holy

Spirit, we will receive clear direction on how to respond to any situation. In the case of Job, God was teaching him about wisdom. Knowing what to do in any situation is vital.

Let us all remember to ask God for wisdom. Let us not be arrogant and self-directed. The book of proverbs, which is considered the book of wisdom, instructs us to trust in the Lord with all of our heart and not to lean to our own understanding, but acknowledge God in our ways and God will direct our paths, Proverbs 3:5, 6. It should feel really good when we take charge of our lives by the leading of the Holy Scriptures. Also, resting in the awesome assurance that our lives are safe in the loving hands of God through Jesus Christ our Savior. The Psalmist David said "Oh taste and see that the Lord is good.

Our Gods' peace is so good and his son Jesus is the Prince of peace... isn't that cool? David the Psalmist shared these profound words, "I will both lay me down in peace and sleep for thou Lord only makes me dwell in safety ', (Psalm 4:8). Let me challenge you my reader to look for people who possess a life of peace. The bible says, "Mark the perfect Man and behold the upright for the end of that man is peace", (Psalm 37:37). I believe that when we embrace the peaceful fruit in our lives, we are giving ourselves permission to trust God. I believe then that we allow ourselves to really live and enjoy life as opposed to just existing. Deciding to accept the fruit of peace is truly a choice. David, the Psalmist had this confession, "I am for Peace..." (Psalm 120:7).

A man of understanding also holds his peace according to Proverbs 11:12. Our peace must become more valuable and precious to us than any circumstance and situation around us. Do you remember what the Lord told the children of Israel? He said that he would fight for them if they held their peace, Exodus 14:14. They were assured that God would be there to fight for them. While we are waiting on God to fight the battle, we should allow ourselves to stay in the love of God with a heart of forgiveness. Training our hearts not to wish evil upon others and to not allow deceit within our hearts. The bible records this verse as such "deceit is in the heart of them that imagine evil; but to the counselors of peace there is joy", (Proverbs 12:20).

Are you a counselor of peace, or confusion? Do you offer hope and healing to people and to the situations around them? When our ways please the Lord, he will cause even our enemies to be at peace with us, Proverbs 16:7. Pleasing God will cause our enemies to take a back seat to the destruction that they thought they could destroy us with. God will cause them to begin to bless us, only because we chose to please God. Our God will always turn the tables for our benefit. Just trust him because our God is so faithful! I get so excited when I think about the Prince of Peace, this is one of the names and characteristics of Jesus, and I love him so much!

The verse in Isaiah 9:6 reads, "For unto us a child is born, unto us a son is given, and the government shall be upon his shoulder; and his name shall be called Wonderful, Counselor, the Mighty God, the Everlasting Father, the Prince of Peace. Jesus admonishes us to have peace with one another, Mark 9:50. My personal philosophy about keeping peace with others is **DO NOT TRIP OVER SOMEONE ELSE'S HUMANITY."**

People will make mistakes and bad choices at times. Our responsibility is to love them, not try to change them. The bible said "Owe no man nothing but to love him." Jesus said to give light to them that sit in darkness and in the shadow of death, we should guide our feet into the way of peace", (Luke 1:79). He also said "My peace I leave with you, my peace I give unto you", (St John 14:27). Our lives can be tranquil on the inside of our hearts. We do not have to be disturbed by the cares of this life. Jesus offered us peace. **PLEASE RECEIVE IT, AND LIVE! (SMILE)!**

Paul the Apostle shared these profound words, "To be spiritually minded is life and peace", (Romans 8:6). Our thoughts must be governed by the Holy Spirit and character of our Creator, God if we want everlasting peace. The bible said that the kingdom of God is peace, Romans 14:17. Therefore, we ought to allow the kingdom of God to reign. We should not entertain and subject ourselves to a life of confusion. According to 1st Corinthians 14:33, "God is not the author of confusion but of peace."

The gospel of Jesus Christ is peace. The word of God records this passage in Ephesians 6:15 that, "we should have our feet shod with the preparation of the gospel of peace". In other words, wherever we go we should take the peace of God with us. Then after we have left their presence, we should have infected the place and the people with the peace of God. I am so Godly proud of myself when I chose to discipline my thinking and disposition to perform my life according to the word of God. The peace of God, then overtakes my mind and my emotional state, and it feels **Soooooo GOOD!** Our God sows a fruit of righteousness within us when we make peace, James 3:18. In other words Gods' character begins to take root in our lives when we chose to do the right thing by faith.

The Holy bible encourages us to seek peace and ensue it, 1st Peter 3:11. I challenge you to go after God's peace as if it is a hidden treasure. Once you find it, please allow it to be your guide.

"Now the God of Peace that brought Jesus from the dead, our Lord Jesus, that great Sheppard of sheep through the blood of the everlasting covenant, make you perfect in every good work to do his will, working in you that which is well pleasing in his sight, through Jesus Christ to whom be glory forever and ever, Amen. Hebrews 13:20, 21).

REFLECTION PAGE

After reading Chapter 9, my reflections are:

1. _____

2. _____

3. _____

I will make a personal commitment to:

1. _____

2. _____

3. _____

Areas I should repent about are:

1. _____

2. _____

3. _____

This chapter affirmed my life in the following areas:

1. _____

2. _____

3. _____

GLOSSARY

Abide - To remain, continue, and stay

Abiding - Continuing without change

Adamant - Utterly unyielding in attitude or opinion

Admonish - To advice or caution; to urge to a duty or remind of an obligation

Amazing - To overwhelm with surprise

Assurance – Promise or guarantee

Attitude - Disposition

Authority - Power to make decisions

Breech - Broken places

Calvary - A hill near ancient Jerusalem where Jesus was crucified

Captive – To be enslaved

Catalyst - A person or thing that precipitates an event or change

Challenge - A call to fight or go after something or someone; to inject

Christian - One who believes in and follows the teachings of Jesus Christ

Components - An element of something

Commitment - Obligation or pledge

Contemplation - Act of looking at and thinking about something long and intensely

Cultivate - To promote the growth of something

Deceit – Fraud or cheating

Declaration - An Announcement

Deprivation - A loss of something

Depths – Quality of being deep

Diagnosed - To analyze the cause or nature of something

Diet - Anything that is habitually done

Diligence - Constant in effort to accomplish something

Discipline – To bring to a state of order and obedience, by training and control

Disobedient - Neglecting and refusing to obey

Disputation – Formal debate in which parties attack and defend a question

Doubt -To be uncertain about something

Encourage - To inspire with courage, hope, or confidence

Establish- To set up permanently

Faith - Belief in God

Fear- To be worried or afraid

Fearful - Feelings of dread, apprehension, or solitude

Flee – To move away from swiftly

Endurance - Lasting quality

Goodness - The state or quality of being good

Hasty -Swift in motion

Inadequacy - Quality of being non-adequate

Inferiority - Feelings of inadequacy, lack of self confidence

Ingredients - Something that enters as an element into a mixture

Intimidation - To inspire with fear

Impression - Indentation

Joy - A strong feeling of happiness and delight

KJV - Acronym for King James Version of the Bible

Lament – Feel or express deep sorrowful grief

Love - Affectionate concern for the wellbeing of others

Meditate - To think about or reflect

Meekness – To be tamed

Patience- Ability or willingness to suppress annoyance when confronted with delay

Peace – Freedom from anxiety

Persistent - Continuing in function or activity

Petition -Prayer or entreaty

Profess - To lay claim to something

Refreshing - Pleasingly

Restore – To re-establish

Revival - An evangelistic service for the purpose of affecting a religious awakening

Model – A person whose behavior is imitated by others

Saints – Persons of exceptional holiness

Salvation - Deliverance of the soul from sin

Satan – The chief adversary of man and the chief evil spirit

Scenario –An outline of a natural or an expected course of events

Stamina- Power to endure

Status- The position of an individual in relation to another

Strength- Power to sustain or resist attack

Superfluity – Excessive amount

Temperance - Self-restraint in one's behavior

Temptation – To entice

Treasure – Anything or person greatly valued or highly prized

Virtue –Righteousness, moral excellence

Vital- Necessary

Weary – Physically or mentally exhausted by hard work

Wisdom – The ability to perceive and determine what is good

9781973612919